LONDON MIDLAND
STEAM
IN RETROSPECT

Ivatt 2–6–2T no. 41240 is seen near Bristol Barrow Road's coaling plant.   31.8.55

LONDON MIDLAND
STEAM
IN RETROSPECT

ERIC SAWFORD

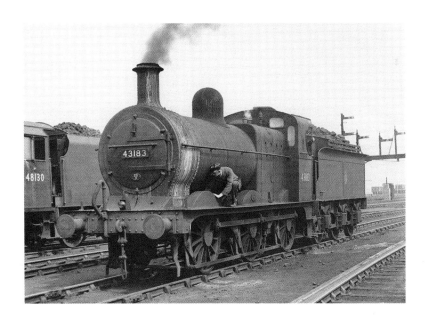

SUTTON PUBLISHING

First published in 2005 by
Sutton Publishing Limited . Phoenix Mill
Thrupp . Stroud . Gloucestershire . GL5 2BU

British Library Cataloguing in Publication Data
A catalogue record for this book is available from the British Library.

ISBN 0-7509-4262-2

Half-title page photograph: Standard class 5 no. 73040, all ready to report for duty at Bolton.   17.3.68

Title page photograph: Johnson 3F 0–6–0 no. 43183 is seen undergoing a driver's inspection before setting off from Normanton depot.   13.5.56

Endpapers. Front: No. 48136 works back to Carlisle, its home depot.   9.63

Back: 8F no. 48607 has just filled up with water and is set to continue its journey south.   5.2.53

Typeset in 10/12pt Palatino.
Typesetting and origination by
Sutton Publishing Limited.
Printed and bound in England by
J.H. Haynes & Co. Ltd, Sparkford.

Contents

Time was running out for the pioneer Midland Compound no. 41000, seen here heading a local passenger train at Kettering. Completed in January 1902, it spent its last years allocated to Derby. It was withdrawn from service in October 1951 but fortunately survives in preservation.   26.5.51

The majority of locomotives allocated to Bedford were 0–6–0s, which were used for shunting and trip workings from nearby brick-works, but a single 8F, no. 48177, was also based at the depot. Here several engines receive attention, having just arrived back after their day's work.   21.8.54

Introduction

The London Midland Region enjoyed many excellent locomotive designs, but one class that will always remain in my memory comprised the sturdy 0–8–0s originating from the London & North Western Railway. These veterans had a long and, in some cases, complicated history. In the early 1950s I was to become very familiar with one engine that certainly came into this category. No. 48898 of Bletchley shed started its life in 1903 as a B class 4-cylinder 0–8–0, being rebuilt just three years later as an F class 4-cylinder Compound 2–8–0. In 1923 it was rebuilt again as a G1 class 0–8–0, being upgraded to G2A in March 1942. This engine was withdrawn in 1962, just six years before steam finished on British Railways. Its service life of fifty-nine years must be among the record-holders for a heavy goods locomotive.

The ex-LNWR 0–8–0s allocated to Bletchley included among their duties sand trains from Leighton Buzzard, and I well recall these engines producing their characteristic wheezing and groaning sounds as they started out on their journey. Among experienced enginemen they were well liked and regarded as 'good pullers'. In their heyday they were of course the principal goods engines of the LNWR, but a considerable number passed into British Railways ownership, and continued in service for several years.

The surviving ex-LNWR passenger engines were not so fortunate, the last being withdrawn in the early 1950s. Only a small number of this company's tank engines survived into BR ownership, among them the 2–4–2Ts with their distinctive tall chimneys. Those that remained were used on branch line trains, and in most cases were replaced by the Ivatt 2MT 2–6–2Ts. The surviving ex-LNWR 0–6–0 tender engines consisted of a few 'coal engines', a Webb 1873 design and the slightly later 'Cauliflowers'. The few remaining examples of the 0–6–2Ts known as 'coal tanks', a tank version of the tender engines, were also soon replaced by more modern motive power.

The London Midland Region was responsible for huge quantities of goods traffic, particularly coal from the many pits in the area. In 1927 the first Beyer-Garratt 2–6–6–2T appeared. These engines were principally used to haul coal and iron ore on the Midland main line and later shared this work with Stanier 8F 2–8–0s. The last of the Garratts was withdrawn in 1958, by which time the Standard 9F 2–10–0s had already taken over many of their duties.

A glance at a railway map of the early 1950s soon reveals the numerous cross-country and branch lines that existed at that time, many of which were to close before the end of the decade. The London Midland Region was no exception. Such services were often the domain of veterans coming to the end of their working lives. Cross-country lines were frequently worked by 2P 4–4–0s, with a few class 5s responsible for the heavier trains. The arrival of diesel multiple units dramatically reduced the number of steam locomotives required and many depots soon had a row of engines in store that would never work again.

Only on one occasion did I have the opportunity of photographing the massive 0–10–0 no. 58100 banking on the famous Lickey incline. Allocated to Bromsgrove shed, this engine spent its entire working life on this duty. Built by the Midland Railway in 1919 to the design of Henry Fowler, it travelled to and from Derby works when general overhaul or heavy repairs were required. It was a sad day in 1955 when it was withdrawn, and unfortunately

The first five Ivatt 2MT 2–6–0s were sent to Kettering to replace the veteran Midland 2F 0–6–0s working the Cambridge trains. Three more eventually followed, plus two of the Standard class 2 version. No. 46444 is seen here on the climb up to Huntingdon no. 1 box. London Midland Region territory extended as far as Godmanchester.   24.4.56

this unique engine has not survived into preservation. For many years other engines were also used as bankers on Lickey. In the early days they included 'Jinty' 3F 0–6–0Ts, working in pairs, or more, as required, but in due course other locomotives were employed on this work, Standard 9F 2–10–0s and Western Region panniers among them.

Another good place to see engines working hard was Shap. Some trains could deal with this notorious incline unaided but others, especially the goods engines, often required the services of a banker. These were based at Tebay and consisted of 2–6–4Ts. Enthusiasts waiting patiently in the quiet isolation of Shap Fells could hear a heavy freight set out from Tebay, some miles away and then come to grips with the bank, with both the train engine and the banker blasting away. As soon as it reached a certain point the banker would leave, cross to the Up line and run back light engine to Tebay to await its next duty.

The Midland Railway operated a small engine policy. Its principal passenger trains were worked by 4–4–0s and its heavy goods by 0–6–0s, so double-heading was commonplace. At the formation of the 'Big Four' the LMS also took over many other locomotives with differing wheel arrangements. Its 0–6–0s ranged from the 2Fs introduced in 1875 to numerous 3Fs designed by Johnson & Deeley and the 4Fs which made their debut in 1911 to the design of Henry Fowler. So successful was the latter class that in 1924 the LMS introduced a post-Grouping development with reduced boiler mountings, lower boiler pressure and smaller driving wheels. Despite these modifications the tractive effort remained the same.

Class 5 no. 45438 at Llandudno. Note the separate dome and top feed. Commonly known as 'Black Fives', these engines had 6ft driving wheels and were capable of a fair turn of speed when used on express trains. 16.6.63

The Lancashire & Yorkshire Railway still had a considerable number of locomotives in service when British Railways took over in 1948. The majority were 0–6–0s, and the few remaining 0–8–0s were soon withdrawn, as were the last 4–6–0s. Shunting locomotives consisted of a sizeable number of 0–6–0STs; these were rebuilds by John Aspinall of an early 0–6–0 design. They were distributed among a number of sheds with five allocated to Horwich works for shunting duties; these retained their LMS numbers.

Small short-wheelbase tank locomotives were to be found on all regions. The Lancashire & Yorkshire contributed over twenty small 0–4–0STs; some of these were to be found a long way from their home territory, Derby and Bristol, for example, using them as shed pilots. The Midland Railway also contributed ten 0–4–0Ts and a small number of 0–4–0STs. In 1932 the well-known company Kitson of Leeds supplied five neat 0–4–0STs to the LMS. Over twenty years later BR built a further five at their Horwich works, four being completed in 1953, the last one in January 1954. A considerable number of ex-Lancashire & Yorkshire 2–4–2Ts were taken into British Railways stock, and as might be expected there were several variations among them. These locomotives were principally used on branch lines in the northern counties. Having said that, on occasions the engines were also allocated to depots a considerable distance from their home territory. One of these was Wellingborough, where they worked a local branch until replaced by Standard class 2MT 2–6–2Ts.

Ex-Lancashire & Yorkshire 0–6–0s were for many years a familiar sight in the north, and also away from home territory on the North Wales coast line. Examples were to be found at

Llandudno. Junction, Rhyl and Bangor, in some cases replacing veteran ex-LNWR 0–6–0s on withdrawal. Other sheds that had these engines at various times included Birkenhead, Edge Hill, Warrington, Speke Junction and Nottingham.

In 1946 Ivatt introduced the highly successful lightweight 2–6–0s of the 64XX series, which were designed to replace ageing locomotives on cross-country routes. The first depot to receive them was Kettering, and their arrival completely changed the Cambridge service which was at that time in the hands of veteran ex-Midland 0–6–0s. The new 2–6–0s immediately became popular with the Kettering enginemen, their comfortable cabs and other refinements being particularly welcome. As the new engines were delivered, 2Fs in store became a familiar sight, either in sidings or left at the back of the shed.

Goods traffic on the Cambridge line was very sparse, although a daily pick-up goods ran to Godmanchester, at the end of LMR territory. In the summer months a heavy fruit train used the line on its way to the northern markets. The ex-Midland 0–6–0s continued to work these trains until sufficient numbers of the new Ivatt engines became available. The line had severe weight and speed restrictions between St Ives and Huntingdon East because of wooden trestle bridges. A single engine was responsible for the trains as far as Huntingdon East, where a pilot was waiting to help it over the steeply graded route to Kettering. On occasions the train could have fifty or so loaded vans, which caused the unaided 2Fs to really struggle. Several times I witnessed this on the curve before the Huntingdon East station. The train would be almost at a standstill, with the fireman walking in front of the engine and throwing grit on to the tracks to help with traction. Even so, the veteran 2F would be slipping violently and sending a plume of smoke and cinders high into the air. Somehow, though, they always made it, and after negotiating another sharp curve with its check rails and 10mph speed restriction they reached the waiting pilot. Even when the new Ivatts took over these services completely a pilot was still necessary for the section through to Kettering.

Such was the success of Ivatt's 2–6–0 design that these engines eventually found their way to other regions. This also applied to the 2–6–2 tank version of the 12XX (later 412XX) series, which also made their debut in the same year. Both designs resulted in many older engines being withdrawn and scrapped.

The introduction of the British Railways Standard designs resulted in many changes, especially as their numbers built up by the mid-1950s. The Bedford to St Pancras local service, for example, was for years in the hands of 3-cylinder Compound 4P 4–4–0s allocated to Bedford depot, but in due course Standard 4MT 4–6–0s and 4MT 2–6–4Ts took over these duties. Initially a number of Compounds were placed in store, but most never worked again and eventually made their last journey to Derby works for scrapping. (This was before the days of private companies cutting up withdrawn locomotives.)

So far little mention has been made of the more modern locomotives that powered London Midland services. These were the products of Sir William Stanier, Chief Mechanical Engineer of the LMS between 1932 and 1944, who introduced several classic designs. In 1934 the first taper-boiler 5MT 4–6–0s appeared. These powerful locomotives were capable of handling express trains but were equally at home on many other duties. In all, 842 were built over a long period; many lasted to the very end of BR steam, among them a number of experimental locomotives, such as one with Stephenson link motion, roller-bearings and double chimneys. Others were fitted with Caprotti valve gear and roller-bearings, in some cases with double chimneys, while a batch of ten had steel fireboxes. The following year (1935) another classic taper-boiler design appeared, this time for heavy freight. The 8F 2–8–0s were built not only for the LMS but also for war service, and after the end of hostilities some were to end their working lives a long way from Britain.

In 1933 Stanier turned his attention to express passenger locomotives and introduced the 13-strong 'Princess Royal' class, followed a year later by the 'Jubilee' class, a 6P design. But it was in 1937 that Stanier's masterpiece appeared, in the shape of the magnificent 'Princess Coronation' class Pacifics. In total 38 were built, some of which were originally streamlined.

'Jubilee' class no. 45738 *Samson* heads a Wolverhampton to London Euston express through Bletchley. This engine was one of nine 'Jubilees' allocated to 3B Bushbury depot, an ex-LNWR shed. 5.9.54

For thirty-seven years this massive 0–10–0 banked both passenger and goods trains on the famous Lickey incline. Built at Derby works in 1919 to the design of H. Fowler, it was allocated to Bromsgrove depot. This huge four-cylinder engine, widely known as 'Big Bertha', weighed just over 73 tons and had a tractive effort of 43315lb; unfortunately it has not survived into preservation. 17.5.55

The last two, no. 46256 *Sir William Stanier FRS* and no. 46257 *City of Salford*, were completed in May 1948, five months after nationalisation. Both had roller-bearings and detail differences, and were allocated to Camden depot in the mid-1950s. Both were withdrawn in 1964. The streamlined locomotives later had the casing removed; these were recognisable by the tapered top to the smokebox.

During his time as Chief Mechanical Engineer of the LMS Sir William Stanier also turned his attention to other locomotive types required for a wide range of duties. His tank engines included a 2–6–2T taper-boiler 3MT design in 1935 and the very useful 4MT 2–6–4T. One tank class that received very little attention was the ten 2P 0–4–4Ts introduced just after he took up his appointment in 1932. Just before the class 5 4–6–0s made their debut, Stanier introduced a 2–6–0 design, also 5MT. These were occasionally seen on passenger work but more often on goods, especially in later years. All of these classes were taken into London Midland stock, except those locomotives that had been allocated to Scottish depots in LMS days; these were taken over by the Scottish Region.

In the early 1950s Crewe works relied on a fascinating selection of engines to carry out shunting work. There was a solitary example of the Webb 0–6–0ST design introduced in 1870, which still carried its LNWR number 3323. Four more of these veterans were to be found at Wolverton carriage works. Also at Crewe were the last two examples of an 0–4–2T design known as Bissel trucks. Withdrawn ex-LNWR 0–6–0 engines from the 'Coal' and 'Cauliflower' classes also shunted wagons at Crewe before they too eventually fell victim to the scrapman's cutting torch. Perhaps the strangest of all the locomotives to be found at Crewe was an ex-Caledonian Railway 'Pug', 0–4–0ST no. 56032.

In this book it is possible to give only a brief outline of the London Midland Region and its locomotives, but the accompanying pictures show a wide representation of what was around in steam days. Unquestionably the heyday of steam was the period from nationalisation in 1948 to 1955; certainly this was the most interesting time for enthusiasts, although sadly many famous classes became extinct within this period. Some of the photographs taken in 1950/1 were on long-obsolete film sizes. It was not a good time for railway photography: film was scarce and of much slower speeds than that available today. In 1953 I purchased an Agfa Isolette camera which produced twelve 2¼in square negatives on 120 film, and this was to become my faithful companion for many years.

1. Passenger Locomotives

Two years after the LNER's famous A4 class engines made their debut in 1935, Sir William Stanier introduced his improved LMS Pacific design known as the 'Princess Coronation' class (but widely referred to as the 'Duchess' class). The new engines were designed to haul a new high-speed Anglo-Scottish train known as the 'Coronation Scot' but would also work other express trains on what were referred to as 'XL' schedules. Five of the new engines, all of them streamlined, were completed at Crewe in 1937. This design, the last to be introduced by Sir William Stanier, was unquestionably his masterpiece. They soon proved to be highly successful and powerful locomotives. Twenty-four members of the class were built streamlined, although in 1946/7 all but one had the casing removed. (No. 46243 retained it until May 1949.) The final locomotive, no. 46257 *City of Salford* was completed in May 1948, several months into BR days. This and the penultimate engine, no. 46256 *Sir William A. Stanier FRS*, were an Ivatt development having detail alterations and roller-bearings. Withdrawals of the class commenced in 1962, with the last going in 1964.

In 1932 the LMS passenger locomotives, especially the ex-LNWR 'Claughtons', were far from satisfactory. Two years later Stanier introduced his famous class 5 4–6–0s and also the 'Jubilee' class, a taper-boiler development of the 'Patriot' class. In total, 191 'Jubilees' were built at Crewe and Derby and by the North British Locomotive Company. Teething problems were soon resolved and the 'Jubilees' proved themselves to be good intermediate express locomotives.

The following year Stanier introduced his 13-strong 'Princess Royal' class, all of which were built at Crewe. Among them was an experimental engine known as the 'Turbomotive', which was rebuilt in 1952 and withdrawn in 1954 following an accident. Happily two 'Princess Royal' and three 'Princess Coronation' engines have been preserved.

When British Railways was formed in 1948 the passenger locomotives of the London Midland Region were principally Stanier designs, with Compounds and 2P 4–4–0s on secondary services. The last of the LNWR passenger locomotive designs were withdrawn shortly after nationalisation.

The Up 'Royal Scot' slows to run through Rugby station headed by 'Princess Coronation' no. 46247 *City of Liverpool* working home from Glasgow. Unlike today's journeys, there was plenty to interest the enthusiast in the 1950s, so long runs were far from boring.   29.5.54

Opposite, top: A popular spot for enthusiasts was to the north end of Bletchley station, and it was from there that this photograph was taken of no. 46248 *City of Leeds* heading for London with an express. This engine was completed at Crewe works in October 1943, one of four that made their debut that year. It remained in service until September 1964.   5.9.54

Opposite, bottom: 'Princess Coronation' class no. 46245 *City of London* presented a sorry sight standing in the works yard at Crewe. Two sets of driving wheels had been removed, together with other parts. In the background are the frames of a class 5.   14.8.52

'Britannia' class no. 70031 *Lord Byron* arrives at Rugby with an express from Manchester. After a number of years at Longsight depot this engine moved to Aston, whereafter it spent short periods at Willesden and Crewe (North and South) before ending up at Carlisle in company with many other members of the class. 29.5.54

Opposite, top: Five members of the 'Princess Royal' class were allocated to Edge Hill Liverpool depot and were normally to be found on London services. Here no. 46204 *Princess Louise* approaches Rugby on its way to the capital. This engine was withdrawn in October 1961, and after a fairly short period in store it was cut up at Crewe works in May 1962. 29.5.54

Opposite, bottom: Another picture of no. 46204 *Princess Louise*, this time thundering through Bletchley with a heavy Liverpool express. 5.9.54

By 1966 most of the 'Britannias' were in a very run-down condition. No. 70016 *Ariel*, a Carlisle engine, is seen here at Leeds Holbeck. It had lost its nameplates, but surprisingly the front number and shedplate still remained. 20.3.66

By 1967 Crewe South shed was a shadow of its former self, although steam was still very much in evidence. Here 'Britannia' class no. 70024 *Vulcan* moves carefully off the turntable. Like most of the class, this locomotive had already lost its nameplates. In some cases the names were simply painted on the windshield.   16.10.66

'Britannia' class no. 70022 *Tornado*. In the mid-1950s this engine was allocated to Newton Abbot depot, where it was the only member of the class, although others were to be found at Old Oak Common and Cardiff Canton. Many members of the class ended their days on the London Midland Region. No. 70022 is seen here at Crewe South, its name painted neatly on the side to replace the missing nameplate.   16.10.66

This 'Royal Scot', no. 46147 *The Northamptonshire Regiment*, was one of those allocated to Camden depot. It is seen here leaving Chester with a Holyhead express, with the busy yards of Chester shed visible on the right. 12.8.52

Ex-works engines were often to be seen at Crewe North prior to their return to their home depot. Camden-based 'Royal Scot' no. 46143 *The South Staffordshire Regiment* is seen here. Note that the tender is still lettered 'British Railways', and that the engine has still to be fitted with windshields. 12.8.52

'Royal Scot' no. 46134 *The Cheshire Regiment* heads a long parcel train at Rugby. For several years this engine was allocated to Crewe North, ending its days at Carlisle from where it was withdrawn in November 1962.   29.5.54

Opposite, top: 'Royal Scot' no. 46122 *Royal Ulster Rifleman* heading the 'Mancunian'. Members of this class and the 'Jubilees' allocated to Longsight depot were responsible for the London services. Bletchley depot is to the left of this picture.   5.9.54

Opposite, bottom: 'Royal Scot' no. 46111 *Royal Fusilier* was a Longsight engine that had presumably failed on a Manchester train, since it ended up for repairs in the cramped conditions of Bletchley depot. The 'Not to be moved' sign is prominently displayed on its cabside.   5.9.54

During the 1960s Llandudno had a number of large passenger engines in its allocation, one of which was 'Royal Scot' no. 46155 *The Lancer*. This engine was allocated to the shed for ten months before moving to Crewe North; it ended its days at Carlisle. 9.6.63

Opposite, top: Rebuilt 'Patriot' no. 45534 *E. Tootal Broadhurst* of Edge Hill depot heading a Liverpool express. This engine was rebuilt in December 1948 and remained in service until May 1964. It was withdrawn from Crewe North and cut up at the works the following month. 29.4.56

Opposite, bottom: In the early 1960s Llandudno Junction shed had an allocation of just over twenty engines. One of the most interesting was rebuilt 'Patriot' class no. 45534 *E. Tootal Broadhurst*, seen in the centre of this picture. This was for years an Edge Hill locomotive, but it also worked from several other depots, in the process spending two periods at Llandudno. Alongside is 3F 0–6–0T no. 47669 and a Standard class 4 4–6–0. 9.6.63

Rebuilt 'Jubilee' no. 45735 *Comet*, a Camden engine, stands at Llandudno with an early morning London train. Two 'Jubilees' were rebuilt with larger boilers and double chimneys and reclassified 7P. No. 45735 was withdrawn in 1964 and after just three months in store was cut up by Cashmores.   14.8.52

Opposite, top: During the 1950s 'Jubilee' class locomotives were in charge of the principal express trains on the Midland main line. Here is no. 45621 *Northern Rhodesia* at St Pancras with a full head of steam.   7.7.51

Opposite, bottom: The fireman relaxes for a few minutes as 'Jubilee' class no. 45595 *Southern Rhodesia* approaches Bletchley station heading a Euston-bound special. Bletchley was an important junction, with services to Cambridge and Oxford.   5.9.54

With a 'Not to be moved' sign on its cab, 'Jubilee' no. 45737 *Atlas* awaits attention at Bletchley. Note the improvised bench complete with vice and what passed for doors.
5.9.54

Opposite, top: 'Jubilee' class no. 45631 *Tanganyika* of Longsight depot takes water at Aston prior to its return working. Over a two-year period 191 members of the class were built at Crewe, Derby and at the North British Locomotive Company works.
17.7.55

Opposite, bottom: 'Jubilee' class locomotives from Kentish Town were a familiar sight at Trafford Park. Here no. 45614 *Leeward Islands* is being made ready for its return journey to London. A considerable amount of ash still remains on the front running plate, but no doubt this would have been removed before the engine left the depot.
22.9.57

'Jubilee' class no. 45581 *Bihar and Orissa* was one of five members of the class allocated to Farnley Junction shed. This engine was one of a batch built by the North British Locomotive Company and completed in October 1934. It remained in service until August 1966.   13.5.56

Opposite, top: On a grey day with heavy showers 'Jubilee' class no. 45741 *Leinster* arrives at Rugby with an express from Birmingham. This engine was one of the last batch of five completed in December 1936 at Crewe works. Withdrawal was in January 1964, and it ended its days at Crewe in April the same year.   29.5.54

Opposite, bottom: Willesden depot had three 'Patriot' class locomotives in its allocation, one of which, no. 45546 *Fleetwood*, is seen here at Crewe North. This engine was completed at Crewe in March 1934 and withdrawn in June 1962. In their final years the 'Patriots' were mostly seen on parcel and excursion trains.   12.8.52

'Patriot' class no. 45500 *Patriot* and sister engine *St Dunstans* were rebuilds of LNWR 'Claughtons' no. 5971 and no. 5902, but retaining the original wheels and other details. *Patriot* was completed at Derby works in November 1930. Seen here at Trafford Park, it had just worked in from Carlisle. 22.9.57

Several of the unrebuilt 'Patriot' class 4–6–0s were never named. No. 45517, photographed leaving Camden shed, was one of them. In the summer months these engines were often seen on parcels and fast goods trains as well as excursions and relief services. Note the interesting points in the foreground. 13.11.55

Unrebuilt 'Patriot' class locomotive no. 45543 *Home Guard* is seen here at Crewe North. Built in 1934, it completed twenty-nine years' service. Eighteen members of this class were rebuilt.   12.8.52

For many years Midland Compound 4–4–0s worked local services from Bedford to St Pancras but eventually British Railways Standard 4MT 2–6–4Ts and class 4MT 4–6–0s took over these duties. Here no. 41049 arrives on shed at Bedford, having worked in from London. This engine was withdrawn in March 1959.   11.9.54

During the early 1950s Chester depot had eleven Compound 4–4–0s on its books, including nos 41153 and 41106, seen here awaiting their next duties. These engines were principally employed on local services in the area.   12.8.52

Opposite, top: Having just worked in to Chester, 2P 4–4–0 no. 40629 arrives on shed for coal and water. The engine was lined out and carried on its tender the words 'British Railways', soon to be replaced with an emblem.   12.8.52

Opposite, bottom: During the summer months large numbers of excursion and special trains arrived in the North Wales resorts from many parts of the country. Compound no. 41114, seen here heading a special at Rhyl, was a Llandudno Junction engine at this time.   10.8.52

Still with its tender lettered 'LMS', Compound no. 41086 heads an early morning express service at Llandudno. This engine was allocated to Llandudno Junction depot at this time, and remained in service until May 1958.   14.8.52

Opposite, top: Compound no. 41106 stands ready for the road at Chester, its tender simply lettered 'British Railways'. This locomotive was completed at Derby in November 1925 and remained in service until July 1958. Many of the remaining Compounds were withdrawn in the late 1950s, just two surviving into 1960.   12.8.52

Opposite, bottom: Compound no. 41054 runs over the scissors crossing at the approach to Bedford locomotive depot. The days of these engines on the St Pancras service were numbered, as within a short time these duties would be taken over by BR Standard 4MTs.   21.8.54

The introduction of a steady stream of British Railways Standard designs resulted in many veterans being placed in store. Compound no. 41116 was officially withdrawn three months after this picture was taken at Trafford Park, and it is unlikely that it ever worked again.   22.9.57

Opposite, top: During the early 1950s massive inroads were made into the LMS-built Compounds. No. 41096 was nearing the end of its days when photographed at Nottingham; within a month it would have made its last journey to Derby works, where it was built in 1925.   4.4.54

Opposite, bottom: 2P 4–4–0 no. 40629, a visitor from Rhyl depot, stands ready to be recoaled at Chester. Built in 1930, it was a post-Grouping development of the original Midland design. The differences included 6ft 9in driving wheels and reduced boiler mountings.   12.8.52

The Midland 2P 4–4–0s were capable of a fair turn of speed. Here no. 40526 of Burton shed heads a Leicester train at Walton. In the background is the East Coast main line. These services were soon to be taken over by Standard 4MT 4–6–0s.

14.8.54

During the early 1950s a few of the early 2P 4–4–0s still remained in service. No. 40324, seen here on carriage pilot duties at Llandudno station, had an interesting history. Built for the Somerset & Dorset Railway, it was rebuilt in 1921 and taken into LMS stock in 1930.

14.8.52

2. Mixed Traffic Designs

Sir William Stanier took over as Chief Mechanical Engineer of the LMS in 1932 and one of his priorities was to address the need for a 4–6–0 'maid of all work' mixed traffic locomotive. In 1934 his first new design, the class 5, appeared. They soon became widely known as 'Black Fives'. In all, 842 'Black Fives' were built between 1934 and 1951. When Sir William Stanier retired in 1944 construction was continued by his successors Charles Fairburn and H.G. Ivatt. Owing to the large numbers involved, they were built at several locations, with Crewe, Horwich and Derby all participating, together with the Vulcan Foundry and Armstrong-Whitworth.

At the design stage of the class 5 several important points had to be considered. First, it had to be a straightforward 2-cylinder locomotive, capable of a wide range of duties (including express trains) and able to work over virtually the whole of the LMS network, so size, weight and length were all important factors. In time, the class 5 proved itself a true 'classic', and it was one of the most successful designs ever built for the British railway system.

Unlike the Stanier 8F 2–8–0s, there was considerable variation to be found throughout the class. For example, the top feed positions varied and some later engines appeared with Stephenson link motion, roller-bearings and double chimneys; others were produced with Caprotti valve gear, and some of these also had roller-bearings and double chimneys. One batch of class 5s was even built with steel fireboxes. From 1950 both Timken and Skefco roller-bearings were used. In 1951 Horwich built the last two engines, nos 44686 and 44687. These had Caprotti poppet valve gear, Skefco roller-bearings and double chimneys, and their high running boards and other features gave them a very distinctive appearance. They were withdrawn in 1965 and 1966 respectively. Only four members of the class were named, all after famous Scottish regiments.

In the year before the introduction of the class 5 another 5MT design, the 2–6–0 'Mogul', was introduced by Sir William Stanier. Forty were built at Crewe works in 1933-4. 'Moguls' were sometimes used on local passenger and excursion trains, but more often than not were to be seen on goods workings. Mention must also be made of the Hughes 5MT design widely known as 'Crabs'. Easily recognised by their inclined cylinders, 245 were built in all and were to be found throughout the region working passenger, parcels and fast goods trains; during the summer months they were often used on excursions and specials.

The final design produced by H.G. Ivatt for the LMS was a 4MT 2–6–0 completed at Horwich; this engine's unusual appearance resulted in considerable controversy in the railway press. It had not only a high footplate, but also huge and out-of-proportion double chimneys. The chimney and blast pipe arrangement was far from satisfactory and in due course a more suitable single chimney was fitted. A total of 162 were built, all but the first three in BR days. Construction took place at Horwich, Doncaster and Darlington works. Locomotives of the class were used on passenger trains, especially on the M&GN. Five examples survived into the last year of steam on British Railways.

The pilot engine for the fruit train that ran during the season from the Cambridgeshire fruit-growing district to the northern markets could not join the train until it arrived at Huntingdon East owing to severe weight restrictions on the bridges between St Ives and Huntingdon East. No. 46403 is seen near the small locomotive sub-shed which is now lost beneath the very busy A14.   20.7.52

Ivatt 2MT no. 46496 arrives at Huntingdon East and exchanges the token with the signalman at no. 1 box, which was responsible for both the main line and the branch. The train had climbed up for almost a mile after crossing under the East Coast Main Line on its way from Kettering. Note the two-way signal with concrete post.   8.3.53

Ivatt 2MTs nos 46403 and 46404 arrive at Huntingdon East with the afternoon Kettering–Cambridge service. The lead engine, no. 46403, was the pilot for the seasonal fruit train that ran to the northern markets. It would have a wait of approximately four hours before the arrival of the fruit train. 20.7.52

Ivatt 2MT no. 46455 leaves Keswick with just a brake van on its return journey to Penrith, but no doubt wagons would be picked up on the return journey. This engine had a long association with the Keswick line, having been allocated to Workington in the mid-1950s. 9.63

The Ivatt 2MT was no stranger to Workington shed. The first examples to be allocated there took over some of the duties worked by veteran ex-LNWR 0–6–0 'Cauliflowers'. No. 46410 was completed at Crewe in January 1947 and remained in service until March 1966.
9.63

Ivatt 2MT no. 46449 runs through Rugby at the head of a local goods. This engine was allocated to Penrith so may well have received attention at Rugby works before returning to its home depot.
5.2.53

Only once was I able to photograph the fruit train carrying the produce of the fruit-growing area of Cambridgeshire on its journey to the northern markets. It ran for only a short period in the summer and it was getting late by the time it arrived at Huntingdon, so light conditions were poor. Here 2MT no. 46401 has just crossed the wooden trestle bridge over the River Ouse and is heading for Huntingdon East to pick up a pilot engine.   10.8.54

London Midland territory extended to Godmanchester, and each week day a pick-up goods ran there from Kettering. Here 2MT no. 46496 prepares to leave in the early afternoon on its return journey with just a brake van; doubtless it would have picked up wagons along the way.   16.7.54

The pilot for the fruit train arrived at Huntingdon East in mid-afternoon, and after turning it had to wait for several hours near Huntingdon no. 1 signal box before the train arrived. It could not move into position until the last passenger from Kettering had cleared. This is Standard 2MT no. 78020.   14.8.54

Ivatt class 4MT no. 43135 at Stourton. This engine was completed at Horwich works in December 1951 and withdrawn in October 1966. These engines, with their high running plate and ugly double chimneys, were the subject of much adverse comment when they were introduced. The double chimneys were subsequently replaced with single chimneys.   20.3.66

Some of the Bletchley–Cambridge trains were worked by Bletchley 4MT 4–6–0s. No. 75034 is seen here nearing Sandy station with an afternoon service. Before the introduction of the Standards, the Cambridge services were in the hands of Fairburn & Stanier 2–6–4Ts, and before that veteran ex-LNWR engines. 31.7.54

The Standard class 4 4–6–0s soon proved themselves to be handy, powerful locomotives. In all, 80 were built with single chimneys, although some working on other regions were fitted with double blastpipes which considerably altered their appearance. No. 75037 was one of a number allocated to Bletchley. 5.9.54

Standard 4MT no. 75014, a Patricroft engine, pictured at Chester General. This engine has survived into preservation and often works enthusiasts' specials.   12.8.52

The Hughes 5MT 2–6–0s (widely known as 'Crabs') were capable of a fair turn of speed and were often used on excursion traffic, fast goods and parcel trains. Introduced in 1926, they were widely distributed in the London Midland Region. No. 42769 was a Nottingham locomotive; built in 1927, it remained in service until February 1964. These engines were instantly recognisable from the large boiler and inclined cylinders that gave rise to their nickname.   4.4.54

Opposite, top: 5MT 2–6–0 no. 42931, seen here at Bletchley, was a Willesden engine. 'Crabs' were not often seen at Bletchley depot.
                                                                                    5.9.54

Opposite, bottom: During the summer months excursions and special trains brought many visiting engines to Llandudno. These were serviced at the locomotive depot before their return working. One such visitor was 'Crab' no. 42769, this engine had only eight months left in service before withdrawal.
                                                                                    9.6.63

The George Hughes 5MT 2–6–0 was built under the direction of Henry Fowler and introduced in LMS days. The 5ft 6in driving wheels gave them a fair turn of speed, and as a result they were usually seen on parcels and in the summer months on excursions and specials. No. 42774, seen here at Manningham, has recently had a coat of paint applied to its smokebox and chimney.

13.5.56

Class 5 no. 45004 shunts empty stock at Bletchley, its home depot. Built at Crewe in March 1935, this engine remained in service until September 1966. Class 5s had only been allocated to the depot for a short time when this picture was taken, but they were often seen on Oxford services. When it was built in 1935 this engine would have had a domeless boiler, but this was later changed to a version with a separate dome and top feed.

29.4.56

Class 5 no. 44837 runs into Rugby, its home town, at the head of an express made up of an assortment of stock. Rugby had thirty-eight class 5s in its allocation, responsible for duties on the main line and cross-country routes. 29.5.54

Fitters at Crewe works replacing the cab fittings on class 5 no. 45250 before reuniting it with its tender. Much of this type of work was done outside owing to lack of space; no doubt this was welcome in the summer but very different during the winter.
14.8.52

Early morning at Llandudno station with Caprotti class 5 no. 44740 ready to leave. In the distance Compound no. 41086 heads a local passenger service to Chester. During the 1950s the station was very busy, especially in the summer months.

14.8.52

Opposite, top: Class 5 no. 45204, seen here at Farnsley Junction shed, was one of 327 locomotives of this type built by Armstrong-Whitworth for the LMS. This engine was completed in November 1935 and originally had a domeless boiler. It remained in service for thirty-two years and was withdrawn the year before steam finished on British Railways. 13.5.56

Opposite, bottom: Millhouses depot class 5 no. 44986 with a self-weighing tender at Holbeck shed. Built at Horwich works and completed in October 1946, it remained in service until May 1967.

13.5.56

Fresh from a general overhaul, almost certainly its last, no. 44819 stands in the works yard at Crewe awaiting the return of its tender. This class 5 was completed at Derby in November 1944 and withdrawn in December 1967, just fourteen months after this picture was taken.   16.10.66

During the summer months Llandudno station was especially busy with excursion trains arriving from many parts of the country – and keeping the station pilot hard at work! No. 44836 is seen here heading a regular local early morning service from Llandudno to Crewe, with a young enthusiast who is clearly more interested in being in the picture than in looking at the locomotive.   14.8.52

Opposite, top: Despite a recent general overhaul, Holbeck class 5 no. 44755 soon ran into trouble. It is shown here at Crewe North, its front bogie removed. This engine was one of three built in 1948 with Caprotti valve gear and Timken roller-bearings, with the top feed situated nearer the double chimney. This engine was withdrawn in November 1963.   12.8.53

Opposite, bottom: Without doubt the Stanier class 5 justly deserved to be called 'a classic design'. Only the 8F 2–8–0s exceeded the number built, by just ten. No. 45311 was a Llandudno engine.   16.6.63

Caprotti class 5 no. 44739 in store at Llandudno. A close look at this picture shows how it differs from the more conventional members of the class. It is unlikely that any of the Caprotti engines stored here ever worked again, and if they did it would have been only for a short period of time.   9.6.63

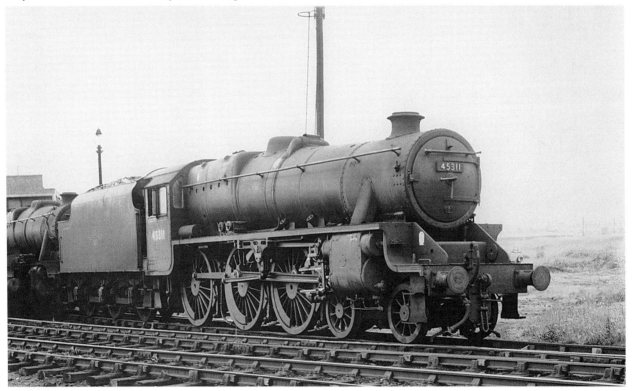

By the mid-1960s Llandudno shed had twenty-two locomotives in its allocation, as opposed to almost forty in the 1950s. Among them were twelve class 5s. No. 45311 was built by Armstrong-Whitworth in February 1937 and was withdrawn in October 1966.   16.6.63

The fireman can relax at last as class 5 no. 45284 heads a train of steel coils on the run down Shap. The bleak, open conditions on Shap are readily apparent in this picture; it's all very splendid in the summer but very different in the winter months.
9.63

Later examples of the class 5 were built with boilers having separate dome and top feed, as in no. 45438 seen here at Llandudno shed. This engine was built by Armstrong-Whitworth and completed in November 1937; it remained in service until August 1966.
16.6.63

Carlisle class 5 no. 45323 blasts up Shap with a fast goods. These engines with their 24455lb tractive effort and 6ft driving wheels were true 'maids of all work' and were equally at home on express passenger work.   9.63

The long climb over Shap certainly made the engines work hard. This is class 5 no. 44937 at the head of a Carlisle express. Bankers were stationed at Tebay to assist heavy goods and passenger trains when necessary.   9.63

Opposite, top: During the 1950s and 1960s many excursion trains ran to Llandudno from all over the country, and quite often the motive power was a class 5 4–6–0. No. 44769 is pictured at the Junction shed awaiting its return journey. Time was running out for this locomotive; built in April 1947, it was fitted with an Ivatt-version boiler having the top feed nearer the chimney.   12.7.64

Opposite, bottom: In the 1950s tests on coal consumption were widely carried out. Class 5 no. 44971 is seen here at Crewe North running with a self-weighing tender. Over thirty class 5s were allocated to Crewe North in the early 1950s.   12.8.52

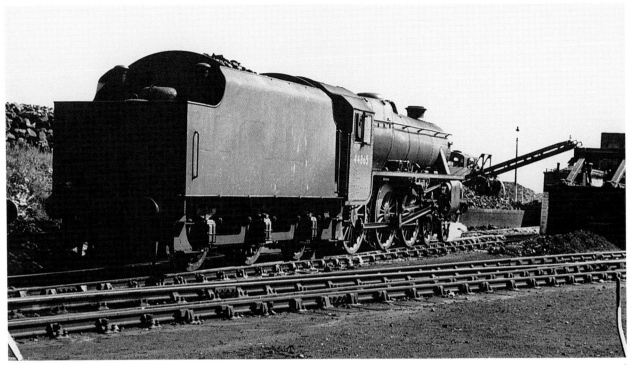

Part of the coaling facilities at Chester can be seen in the background to this study of Class 5 no. 44865. Chester was of reasonable size with forty locomotives on its books; at this time eleven of these were Compounds, along with two 2P 4–4–0s.   12.8.52

You would almost certainly find class 5s at most London Midland depots even if none was allocated, as there was a very strong chance they would arrive as visitors. No. 44928, seen here at Wakefield, was built at Crewe in March 1946. It remained in service until steam finished on British Railways in August 1968.   13.5.56

Holyhead class 5 no. 45247 stands ready to leave Crewe with a local passenger train. Holyhead was not a large shed, but it had 9 class 5s, 6 'Royal Scots' and a number of 'Jinties' in its allocation. 14.8.52

The class 5s were the true workhorses of the London Midland Region. Armstrong-Whitworth built 327 members of the class, including no. 45333, seen here outside its home shed Wellingborough. Completed in March 1937, this engine gave nearly thirty years' service before being withdrawn in June 1966. 18.10.64

The class 5 4–6–0s were built over a long period. They first appeared in 1934, while the last members of the class entered traffic in 1951, well into British Railways days. No. 44828, seen here at Kettering, was built at Crewe and completed in July 1944, remaining in service until September 1967.
18.10.64

Opposite, top: Class 5 no. 44732 was a post-nationalisation engine built at Crewe and completed in February 1949. The top feed in this case is mounted nearer the chimney. A Blackpool engine, it is being prepared at Farnley Junction shed for its return working.
13.5.56

Opposite, bottom: Four Caprotti class 5s were in store at Llandudno shed in mid-1963, including no. 44738, withdrawn in June 1964. The considerable number of variations to be found in the class 5s made them much more interesting to enthusiasts.
9.6.63

It was common for stored locomotives to have their chimneys covered with a piece of tarpaulin, as is the case with no. 44739, seen here at Llandudno. This engine had not been coaled so it was not intended to return to service at short notice. No. 44739 was withdrawn in January 1965.   9.6.63

Opposite, top: The final variant of the class 5 were two Caprotti poppet valve engines, nos 44686 and 44687. The double chimney and raised running boards gave these locomotives a very different appearance. No. 44686 is pictured here in store at Llandudno, its chimney covered in the traditional way. Vandals had already smashed the cab windows.   9.6.63

Opposite, bottom: In 1963 both of the high running place class 5s were to be found in store at Llandudno. No. 44687 was completed at Crewe in May 1951. None of the cab glass remained intact when this picture was taken.   9.6.63

Standard class 5 no. 73031 was brand new and undergoing trials when this picture was taken at Derby. This was one of two engines fitted with Westinghouse brake equipment for working fitted freight trains, but the equipment was later removed. No. 73031 ended its days at Oxford.   10.7.53

Opposite, top: The Standard class 5 4–6–0s soon proved themselves and became well liked by enginemen. Here no. 73002 has its fire cleaned at Derby before being made ready for its next duty.   4.7.51

Opposite, bottom: The Standard class 5s were powerful locomotives with a slightly higher tractive effort than the well-known LMS 'Black Fives'. Introduced in 1951, they soon became a familiar sight on the London Midland and other regions. No. 73094 awaits its next duty at Patricroft.   22.9.57

Two very different class 5 4–6–0s stand side by side at Llandudno Junction shed. Standard no. 73144 was one of the 30-strong batch built at Derby in 1956–7 with Caprotti valve gear. These engines were well liked by enginemen who regarded them as strong locomotives capable of handling all types of work. Alongside is Stanier class 5 no. 45060, which had worked in with a special.   12.7.64

Standard class 5 no. 73099 heads an SMJR rail tour through Bletchley. The six-coach train is composed of Eastern Region Gresley stock. Bletchley motive power depot can just be seen on the left.   29.4.56

3. Heavy Haulage

In the early 1950s the London Midland Region relied principally on two classes for heavy haulage, the Stanier 8F 2–8–0s and the ex-LNWR 0–8–0s, although the latter by that time were more often used on less heavily loaded services. There were of course other classes, such as the 33-strong Beyer-Garratts used on long mineral trains and the Fowler 7F 0–8–0s that were mostly to be found in the north of England. A huge number of 0–6–0s were also in service. In their heyday they were to be found on heavy goods, often double-headed, but in due course they were replaced by larger engines. In later years the 0–6–0s were indispensable for pick-up goods, feeder services and trip working. The majority were ex-Midland Railway or post-Grouping developments, with others of LNWR and Lancashire & Yorkshire Railway origin. The arrival of Standard class 9F 2–10–0s soon changed the scene, the final examples of the Beyer-Garratts going for scrap in 1958. Early in the 1960s the last of the Fowler 7F 0–8–0s, their numbers having been greatly reduced at the end of the 1950s, were withdrawn.

The LMR goods engines that will always remain in my memory were the ex-LNWR 0–8–0s, principally because of the time I spent at Bletchley. This depot had a sizeable number of them in its allocation, and they were used on sand trains and local goods services, at times working through to Cambridge via Bedford and Sandy. Some of these engines had been rebuilt during their long years of service, and a few were running as 2–8–0s during this time. By the 1950s they were starting to show their age and could be instantly identified by their sharp exhaust and wheezing sounds.

As you might expect, a Stanier design was the backbone of LMR goods services, in the shape of the 8F 2–8–0s widely known as 'Eight Freights'. In all 852 were built, all capable of working over most of the lines in the London Midland Region. Introduced in 1935, the design was chosen for military use by the War Department, with many examples going on to provide useful service in distant countries. The introduction of the Standard class 9F 2–10–0s resulted in these powerful engines being allocated to numerous LMR depots.

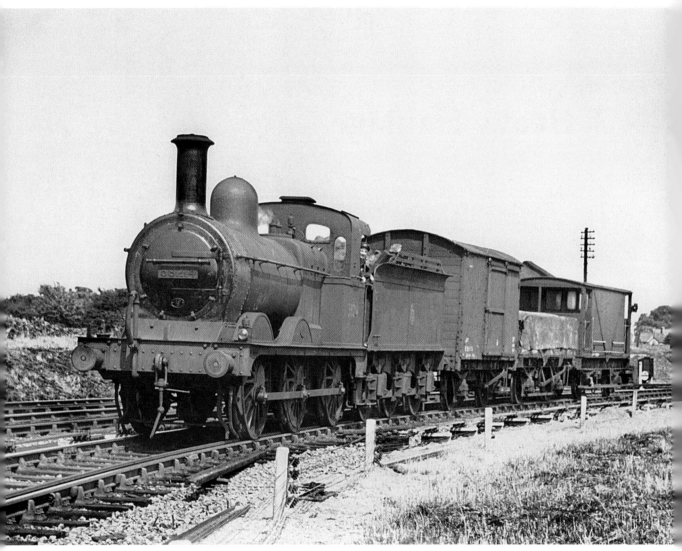

A weekdays only pick-up goods ran between Kettering and Godmanchester. The loading was generally very light, seldom consisting of more than two or three wagons on the final section. Here 2F 0–6–0 no. 58214 passes Huntingdon East on its return journey. As soon as Kettering received enough 2MT 2–6–0s the 2Fs were replaced on this duty.   20.7.52

Opposite, top: Turning a locomotive behind Huntingdon East sub-shed was not easy as the small turntable received very little use. 2F no. 58214 was the engine working the weekdays only pick-up goods.   20.7.52

Opposite, bottom: Standing outside Nottingham shed is 2F no. 58133, one of the class with 4ft 11in driving wheels. Like many other 2Fs, it had been rebuilt with a Belpaire firebox. Only a very small number with round-topped fireboxes remained in service in the early 1950s.   4.4.54

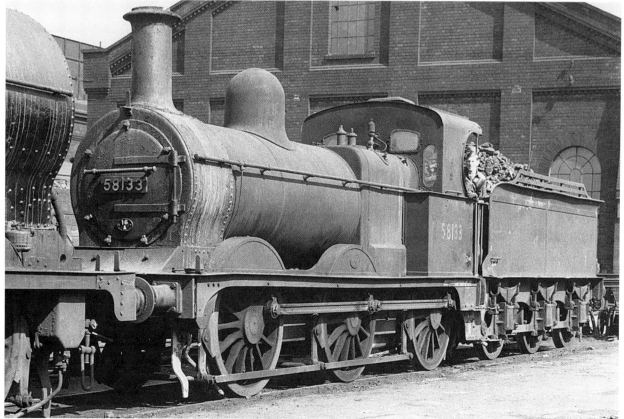

Light conditions were poor when I came across this 2F at Derby. No. 58246 was one of the 1875 design running with round-topped boiler, Salter safety valves and the original cab. Only five were still in this condition during the early 1950s.   10.7.53

Opposite, top: For many years class 2F no. 58173 was a Toton engine. In their heyday these 0–6–0s were the principal goods locomotives on the Midland Railway. This engine was one of those rebuilt with a Belpaire boiler.   4.4.54

Opposite, bottom: Considerable variation was to be found among the ex-Midland Railway 2F 0–6–0s. No. 58197, seen here at Toton, was one of those with 5ft 3in driving wheels. During its long life it, like the majority of its classmates, had been rebuilt with a Belpaire boiler. Toton had a sizeable number of these engines in its allocation in the early 1950s.   4.4.54

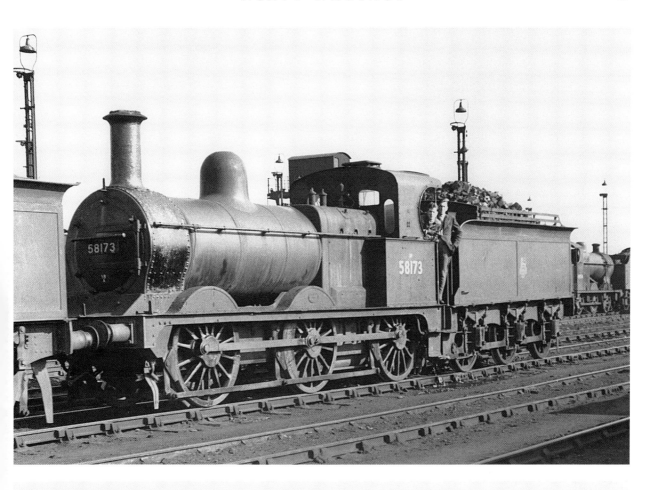

Ex-LNWR 'Coal engine' 0–6–0 no. 58343 at Crewe works. Several examples of the 'Coal' and 'Cauliflower' classes ended up on shunting work here after they had been withdrawn from running stock.
12.8.52

In the early 1950s Rhyl depot had seven ex-Lancashire & Yorkshire 0–6–0s in its allocation but by the end of the decade there were just two as replacement locomotives – all ex-Midland Railway 0–6–0s in the form of two 2Fs and one 3F – were transferred in. No. 52119 was photographed at Llandudno. 9.6.63

A closer view of this locomotive illustrates the clean lines of the design, first introduced by J. Aspinall in 1889. The 0–6–0 tender engines allocated to Rhyl were frequent visitors to Llandudno shed. 9.6.63

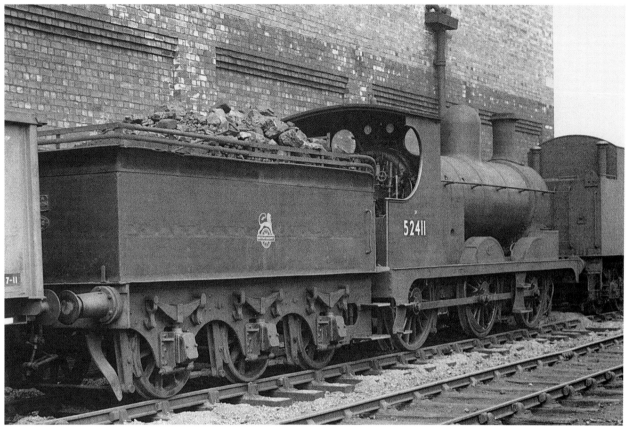

Most of the ex- Lancashire & Yorkshire 0–6–0s were fitted with railed tenders. The one on no. 52411, seen here at Wakefield, appears to have been badly damaged at some time: the effects can be seen along its entire length.   13.5.56

The ex-Lancashire & Yorkshire 0–6–0s were also to be found outside their native territory. No. 52343, seen here at Low Moor, still retained a round-topped boiler, like the majority of its classmates. These engines were first introduced by J. Aspinall in 1889 and became L&Y class 27.   13.5.56

The ex-Lancashire & Yorkshire 0–6–0s introduced in 1889 were widely distributed in the northern counties and were also to be found at considerable distances from home territory. This is no. 52389 at Patricroft. Some members of the class were rebuilt with Belpaire boilers and extended smokeboxes. 22.9.57

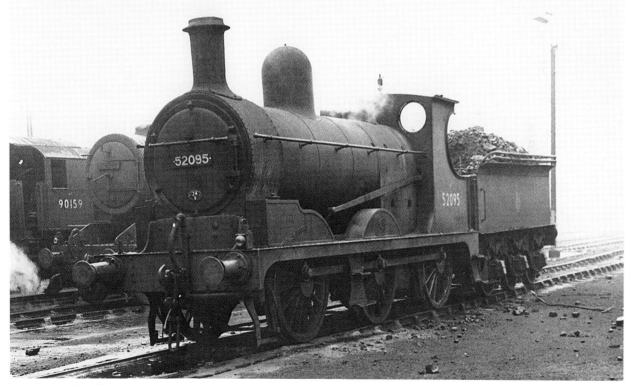

Surrounded by WD 2–8–0s on a dull, wet autumn day at Rose Grove, ex-Lancashire & Yorkshire 0–6–0 no. 52095 was one locomotive I simply had to photograph. In their heyday 0–6–0 tender engines were responsible for much of the goods traffic on the LMS, and double-heading was often necessary, especially if loading was heavy. 22.9.57

From 1911 onwards a fairly small number of the ex-Lancashire & Yorkshire 3F 0–6–0s were rebuilt with Belpaire boilers and extended smokeboxes. No. 52400, seen here at Sowerby Bridge depot, was among them. The rebuilt engines were only 1ton 8cwt heavier than the unrebuilt version.   13.5.56

Opposite, top: Ex-Midland Railway 3F 0–6–0 no. 43618 was allocated to Rhyl depot. It is seen here on a visit to Llandudno. In later years ex-Lancashire & Yorkshire and Midland Railway 0–6–0s could often be found on the North Wales coast line.   9.6.63

Opposite, bottom: Old locomotive tenders in use as water-carriers were a familiar sight at Llandudno. One of these, still lettered LMS, can be seen in front of 3F no. 43618. Two members of the class were allocated to Rhyl at this time.   9.6.63

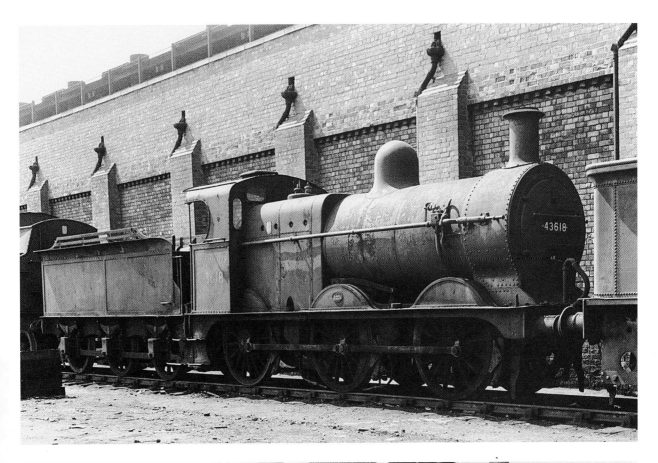

At one time the Midland 3F 0–6–0s were the principal goods locomotives working in conjunction with the earlier 2Fs but by the 1950s they were more often to be found on trip workings and local goods duties. This S.W. Johnson design was introduced in 1885, being rebuilt from 1916 onwards with Belpaire boilers. No. 43579 was one of a number allocated to Stourton depot.   13.5.56

Opposite, top: Stourton (shed code 20B) was originally a Midland Railway depot coming within the Leeds Holbeck district. In its allocation were six 3F 0–6–0s including no. 43392, and these engines had a long association with the shed. Stourton was concerned entirely with goods traffic, having no passenger locomotives in its 50- strong mid-1950s allocation.   13.5.56

Opposite, bottom: The Johnson 3F 0–6–0s were rebuilt with Belpaire boilers by Sir Henry Fowler. No. 43183 is being checked over by its driver before leaving Normanton depot. This engine was one of the few with 4ft 11in driving wheels, the majority having 5ft 3in wheels.   13.5.56

Like many other London Midland Region depots, Bristol Barrow Road had a number of 3F 0–6–0s in its allocation. No. 43712 is seen here coaled and watered ready for its next duty. In the mid-1950s over three hundred 3Fs were still in service.   31.8.55

In 1953 Burton shed had several 3F 0–6–0s that were surplus to requirements. Three had been placed in store in the shed yard, all with their chimneys covered with tarpaulin. On the right is no. 43406, with nos 43423 and 43388 in the background.   10.7.53

Here 4F no. 44035 and no. 44292 await their next duty at Workington. This was an ex-LNWR shed with an allocation of twenty-eight engines in the mid-1950s, including eight 4F 0–6–0s. By 1965 the number of 4Fs had risen to twelve.   9.63

4F no. 44292 at Workington. This design was rugged and powerful, and the locomotives were widely distributed across the London Midland Region. Note the top rails on the tender. 9.63

In 1924 the LMS introduced a post-Grouping development of the earlier Midland 4F design. In all, 580 were built, the last being completed in March 1941. No. 44305, seen here at Workington with a tender cab, was completed at Crewe in October 1926. 9.63

In 1911 Henry Fowler introduced this 4F 0–6–0 design, which proved to be highly successful, the LMS building a further 580 with post-Grouping developments. No. 43960, an ex-Midland Railway engine, is seen here at Stourton although it was in fact a Skipton engine. It was running with a tender cab, which was very welcome to enginemen on duties that involved much tender-first working. 13.5.56

Opposite, top: Fresh from works overhaul, 4F 0–6–0 no. 44094 is back at its home depot, Stourton. This locomotive was one of the post-Grouping developments of the Midland design introduced by the LMS in 1924 and built over a seventeen-year period. Kerr Stuart completed no. 44094 in November 1925; it remained in service until May 1963. 13.5.56

Opposite, bottom: British Railways took over 772 4F 0–6–0s, some of Midland Railway origin, the majority built in LMS days. No. 44577 made its debut in April 1939 and completed twenty-five years' service. It was one of a batch allocated to Nottingham. 4.4.54

4F no. 44562, its tender still lettered 'British Railways', is dwarfed by the massive coaling plant at Nottingham shed. This engine was completed in May 1937 and remained in service until November 1963.

4.4.54

Opposite, top: Having replenished its water supply, 4F no. 44535 leaves the coaling plant at Bedford. This engine was one of the post-Grouping 4Fs, and was completed in September 1928 at Crewe works. It remained in service until September 1963.

21.8.54

Opposite, bottom: The coaling facilities at Kettering involved a considerable amount of hard work with a hopper that was extended and tipped into the locomotive tender, as seen here. No. 43889 was one of the 4F 0–6–0s built by the Midland Railway.

10.7.53

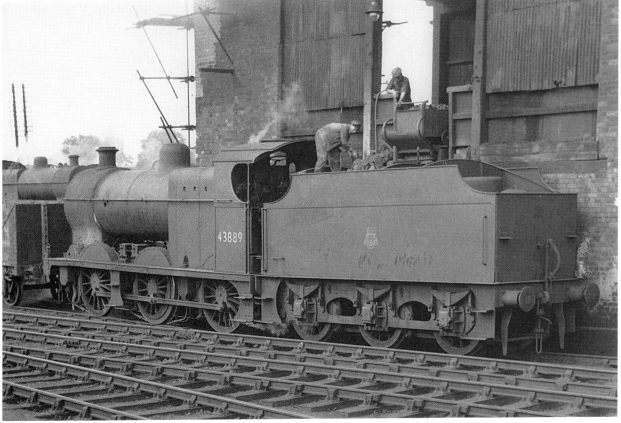

One locomotive type you could be sure of finding at Burton was the 4F 0–6–0. No. 44552 was built at Crewe and completed in December 1928. These engines were true workhorses: this example completed thirty-six years' service.   10.7.53

In 1929 Fowler introduced an 0–8–0 heavy goods locomotive developed from the successful LNWR G2 class. In all, 175 were built at Crewe works over a three-year period. By the mid-1950s fewer than fifty remained in service. No. 49560, pictured at Bolton, was withdrawn two months later.
22.9.57

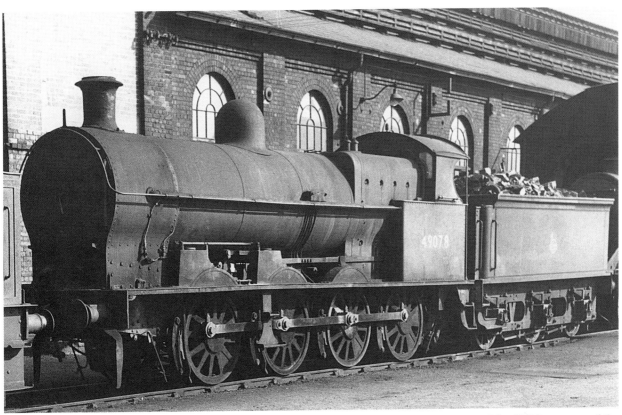

No ex-LNWR 0–8–0s were allocated to Toton, although visiting engines were not uncommon. No. 49078 was one of the latter. This engine started life as a class G; it was later converted to a G1 and in June 1939 to a G2a.   4.4.54

The ex-LNWR 0–8–0s in the Bletchley stud were always great favourites of mine, especially no. 48898 which often worked the Leighton Buzzard sand trains. This particular engine had a long and interesting history which included several rebuilds. It also ran with a tender cab, which can be clearly seen in this picture.   29.4.56

Ex-LNWR 0–8–0 no. 49425 being coaled at Coventry. This was a small shed with just twelve locomotives in its allocation, six of them ex-LNWR 0–8–0s.

5.2.53

Opposite, top: Bletchley shed's no. 49139 was built in September 1910 as a class G; conversion to G1 took place in September 1928. Its final rebuild to G2a came ten years later. By the 1960s the rim of the chimney had certainly seen better days.

15.7.54

Opposite, bottom: No. 49277 was converted to a G2a in August 1947. Here the engine prepares to turn on Bletchley shed turntable. As can be seen, there was little protection for the enginemen in inclement weather conditions, but despite this these locomotives were popular.

15.7.54

Nuneaton depot's 7F 0–8–0 no. 49330 was built as a G1 in 1918 and rebuilt as a G2a in January 1940. In the early 1950s Nuneaton had eighteen of these engines on its books. The engine is pictured here at Bletchley ready for its return journey.

5.9.54

Opposite, top: Austerity WD 2–8–0s were allocated to a number of sheds in the London Midland Region, especially those located in coal-mining districts. No. 90119 was a visitor to Toton, which at this time had 23 Beyer-Garratts and 57 8Fs to handle mineral traffic.

4.4.54

Opposite, bottom: After a general overhaul the WDs' black livery looked very smart but all too soon they took on the appearance of no. 90680, seen here at Huddersfield, its cabside number barely visible through the grime and dirt. Those who knew them in service will remember the WDs by the characteristic clanking sounds they produced.

13.5.56

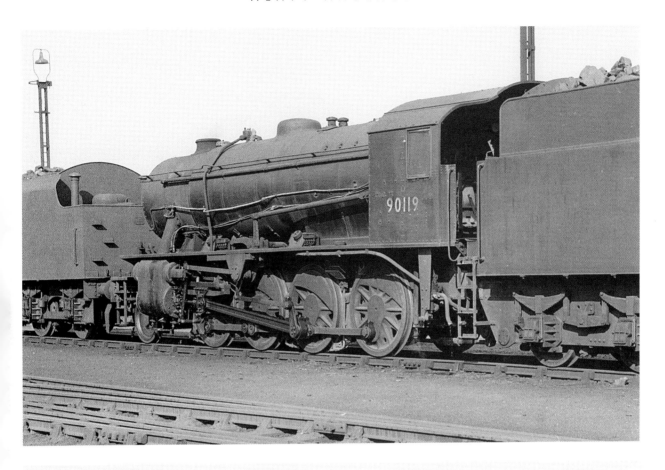

The Ministry of Supply 'Austerity' 2–8–0s were introduced in 1943, and after the war they were offered for sale. In 1948 a large number were purchased by British Railways and they proved to be an invaluable asset. Crewe works had a long association with these engines, and no. 90345 is seen here in the works yard with a classmate.   16.10.66

Opposite, top: Crewe works yard contained a number of withdrawn WD 2–8–0s. No. 90622 had been towed there, its coupling rods removed and its motion tied up.   16.10.66

Opposite, bottom: Most London Midland Region depots had members of the Stanier 8F class in their allocation. No. 48098, seen here at Nottingham, was completed in January 1939 and withdrawn in March 1967. The 8F design was chosen by the Ministry of Supply for war service; many were built new for them, while others already in service were requisitioned for war service and eventually returned after the war over a six-year period.   4.4.54

Kettering depot had twenty Stanier 8F 2–8–0s in its allocation. Among their duties were the iron ore trains originating from quarries at Cranford and the surrounding area. No. 48355 had just arrived on shed from a return working. 11.11.55

Opposite, top: In the mid-1950s Wellingborough shed was home to seventy-eight engines, the majority of them heavy goods, their duties including ironstone traffic from several quarries in the area. As might be expected, a considerable number of 8F 2–8–0s were allocated to the depot but there were also numerous visitors. No. 48456 had recently received a general overhaul; it would not have remained in this smart external condition for long. In addition, a small number of tank engines were allocated for branch line working.   5.2.56

Opposite, bottom: Sundays have always been the day for maintenance and relaying work on the railways. Here 8F no. 48344 heads an engineering train at Northampton. These low-sided wagons were widely used on this type of work.   5.9.54

Awaiting attention, 8F no. 48544 and an ex-LNWR 0–8–0 stand in a siding near Bletchley. Eight 8F 2–8–0s and twelve LNWR 0–8–0s were among the fifty-four engines allocated to the depot.   5.9.54

Opposite, top: Weather conditions were always important for the climb over Shap, especially in the depths of winter. Here 8F no. 48612 is pounding up the gradient with the 2–6–4T banker at the rear doing the same.   9.63

Opposite, bottom: Enthusiasts waiting on Shap could hear a heavy goods train start out from Tebay with both the train engine and the banker working hard. It always seemed quite a while before the train reached you. No. 48136 is working back to its home depot, Carlisle, assisted at the rear by Fairburn 2–6–4T no. 42110.   9.63

8F no. 48549 of Bletchley shed heads a freight from Cambridge through the LMR's Sandy station. From this point the line ran parallel to the East Coast Main Line for a short distance before crossing over it. Considerable goods traffic once used this cross-country route. 31.7.54

Opposite, top: Southbound goods trains often took water at Rugby. 8F no. 48607 has just filled up and is ready to continue its journey. This locomotive was completed at Eastleigh works in September 1943 and remained in service until August 1965. 5.2.53

Opposite, bottom: Having replenished its water supply and with a good head of steam, 8F no. 48607 heads for London, with the coaling tower of Rugby depot in the background. At this time 8Fs were in charge of many heavy goods trains, although the veteran ex-LNWR 0–8–0s were still very much in evidence. 5.2.53

Standard class 9F no. 92123 fresh from a general overhaul. This engine was allocated to Wellingborough but had worked into Kettering, spending Sunday in the almost empty yard. Many locomotives had lost their front number plates by this time, no. 92123 among them.
18.10.64

Franco-Crosti 9F 2–10–0 no. 92026 at Wellingborough. Note the exhaust coming out halfway along the boiler side. What appears to be a normal chimney was in fact only used for lighting up, after which it was closed. The ten Crosti engines suffered many problems and were all rebuilt.   5.2.56

Franco-Crosti 9F 2–10–0 no. 92023 at Birkenhead. In their rebuilt form, these engines retained the original boiler. Owing to its smaller size, they were classified 8F and were never fitted with smoke deflectors. No. 92023 remained in service until 1967.   16.10.66

9F no. 92203 at Crewe South shed, in the typically grubby condition in which many steam locomotives ended their working days. The cabside number is barely visible under the accumulated soot and grime. Some of these engines were built in the early 1960s and had only a short working life.   16.10.66

Northbound goods trains often took on water at Kettering. Beyer-Garratt no. 47980 is seen here heading a train of iron ore wagons from the once-extensive Northamptonshire ironstone quarries. The last of these engines was withdrawn in 1958; many of their duties had been taken over by Standard 9F 2–10–0s.   10.7.53

These massive engines, with their 45,620lb tractive effort, were capable of hauling the heaviest goods trains. All were built by Beyer-Garratt, three in 1927 and the other thirty in 1930; most were later fitted with 10-ton rotating coal-bunkers. No. 47978 was nearing the end of its working life when this picture was taken at Wellingborough. It was withdrawn in March 1957.

        5.2.56

Eastern Region locomotives worked through to Bletchley and Oxford over London Midland Region territory. Here J20 no. 64688 approaches Sandy station after crossing over the East Coast Main Line on its way back to Cambridge. D16 4–4–0s also worked through on passenger services. No. 62585 was a regular visitor on Bletchley shed.

        31.7.54

4. Tank Locomotives

The standard shunting locomotive of the region was the post-Grouping development of an earlier Midland Railway design, known as 'Jinties'. There were 417 later engines plus 60 ex-Midland engines, and their very numbers meant they were found throughout the system.

Local passenger services were principally in the hands of the region's large number of 2–6–4Ts, the earliest 1927 Fowler-design examples being bolstered by others introduced by Stanier and Fairburn. By the mid-1950s work was becoming scarce for the remaining 3P 4–4–2Ts, and examples were to be found in store at several depots. However, a couple of 2–6–2T designs were still to be found on a variety of duties, including local passenger trains and station pilots. These consisted of the 1930 parallel-boiler Fowler design and the Stanier taper-boiler engines introduced in 1935. A number of the former were equipped with condensing apparatus for use on workings to Moorgate in London. In 1946 H.G. Ivatt introduced his 2–6–2T tank version of the 2MT 2–6–0; a total of 130 were built, some of which went to work in other regions. Push-pull services in the region had mostly been in the hands of pre-Grouping veterans. As a result a number of the Ivatt engines were equipped for working these trains.

The pre-Grouping engines consisted of 2–4–2Ts of Lancashire & Yorkshire origin, as well as the 0–4–4Ts introduced by the Midland in 1881. For me the most interesting were the last few remaining ex-LNWR 2–4–2Ts with their very distinctive tall chimneys. Also originating from the LNWR were the last remaining 0–6–2Ts, known as 'coal tanks'. At Wolverton carriage works four Webb-designed 0–6–0STs from 1870 soldiered on, with another (still carrying its LNWR number 3323) to be found at Crewe works. Short-wheelbase tank engines of Lancashire & Yorkshire, Midland and LMS origin were scattered throughout the region, some employed on shunting work where tight curves existed, others used as shed pilots.

Locomotives often ended their days a long way from their original haunts. This was the case with some of the North London Railway 0–6–0Ts, an 1879 design introduced by J.C. Park. Several ended their days working hard on the steeply graded Cromford & High Peak line in Derbyshire.

Seventeen assorted locomotives were used for shunting work at Crewe works in the early 1950s, including this ex-Caledonian Railway 'Pug' no. 56032 (*above*). Behind it is ex-LNWR 0–6–0 no. 58377, which also spent its final days on this work. Another was veteran 0–6–0ST no. 3323 (*below*), a member of the class of 'Special Tanks' introduced by Webb in 1870. At this time it was still carrying its old LNWR number. Four more 'Special Tanks' were to be found at Wolverton carriage works.

12.8.52

Ex-Lancashire & Yorkshire 0–4–0STs were often used as shed pilots. No. 51235 was allocated to Derby and used on this work. These locomotives were introduced by J. Aspinall in 1891 and weighed just over 21 tons. Their short wheelbase also made them ideal for shunting on lines with tight curves. 4.7.51

LNWR 0–6–2T no. 58887 outside Bletchley shed, which was rebuilt in 1953–4. Only a small number of these 0–6–2Ts passed into BR ownership and they were noted for their sharp exhaust, especially when working hard. 6.8.51

Another veteran which I was lucky to see working at Crewe was 'Bissel truck' 0–4–2ST no. 47862. This design was introduced by Webb in 1896. Two passed into BR ownership, both at Crewe. No. 47862 was the last survivor.   14.8.52

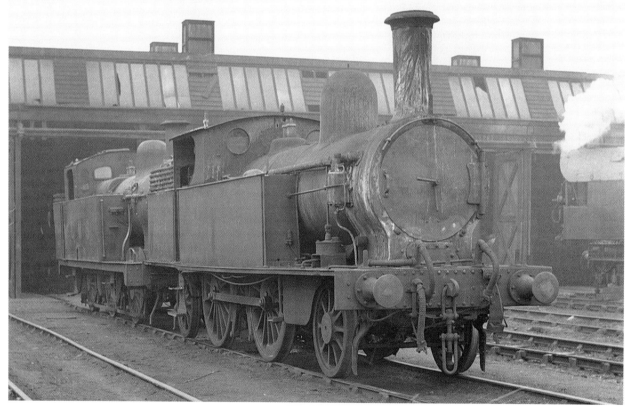

Webb 2–4–2T no. 46654 at Rugby. Just seven months later it was withdrawn from service. Many of these locomotives with their distinctive tall chimneys were fitted for push-pull working, as in this case.
5.2.53

Ex-Midland Railway 1F no. 41661 at Stourton. This design was introduced by S.W. Johnson in 1878 and they were widely known as 'Half Cabs'. Over the years a number of changes took place; some, including this one, were rebuilt with Belpaire boilers, while others received an all-over cab. 13.5.56

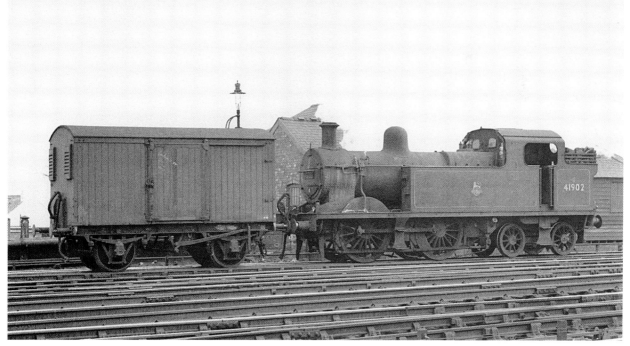

The Stanier 2P 0–4–4Ts were designed to replace older locomotives on push-pull services. By the mid-1950s they were often to be found on station pilot duties. No. 41902 was employed on this work at Bletchley, replacing a 'Jinty'. 29.4.56

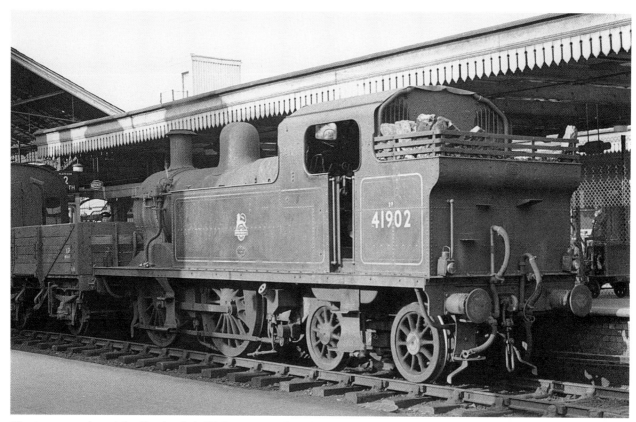

The ten examples of the Stanier 0–4–4T design introduced in 1932 were not particularly well known. All were built at Derby works, nine in 1932 and the last in January 1933. They were designed for push-pull services, but during the 1950s their duties were taken over by more modern designs. No. 41902 had been transferred to Bletchley depot principally for pilot duties. This engine and eight others of the class were withdrawn in 1959, leaving no. 41900 to soldier on until March 1962.

29.4.56

There were several variations of the ex-Lancashire & Yorkshire Railway 2–4–2Ts. No. 50865, pictured here at Huddersfield depot, was one of those with smaller cylinders, longer tanks and larger 4-ton bunker. In 1950 four of these engines were to be found there, but by the mid-1950s there were only two. As with other pre-Grouping tank engines, their duties were being taken over by Ivatt and other 2–6–2Ts. No. 50865 was fitted for push-pull working.   13.5.56

The end of the road for ex-Lancashire & Yorkshire 2–4–2T no. 50752, seen here at Horwich works, after many years' service. This engine was among those of the class with smaller cylinders. Over one hundred ex-Lancashire & Yorkshire 2–4–2Ts were taken into British Railways stock, withdrawals taking place at an ever-increasing rate.   22.9.57

Opposite, top: Three ex-Lancashire & Yorkshire 2P 2–4–2Ts, including no. 50646 (seen here at Bedford), were sent to Wellingborough for branch line passenger working. This engine, which was fitted to work motor trains, retained its 2-ton coal capacity; some had been rebuilt to carry twice this amount.   23.3.56

Opposite, bottom: Over a nine year period 230 of these 0–6–0STs were rebuilt from Barton Wright 0–6–0 tender locomotives and became the standard shunting engines of the Lancashire & Yorkshire Railway. More than one hundred were still in service on nationalisation. No. 51486 was photographed on a grey day at Bolton depot.   16.10.55

Judging by the appearance of the smokebox, chimney, wheels and coupling rods, no. 51445 had recently received works attention, after which the number had been cleaned but not the rest of the engine. Seen here at Bolton, this Edge Hill engine was waiting to work back to its home depot.   22.9.57

The introduction of the very successful H.G. Ivatt 2–6–2T design in 1946 soon resulted in many older locomotives being displaced on branch line duties. No. 41247, photographed at Manningham, was fitted with the LMS short chimney; engines built from 1951 onwards had a longer type.   13.5.56

In the mid-1950s Bristol Barrow Road depot had just one of these Ivatt 2–6–2Ts (no. 41240) in its allocation. In 1958, when this shed became part of the Western Region, three of these Ivatts were still allocated there, including no. 41240, seen here near the massive coaling plant.   31.8.55

The Ivatt 2MTs at Bedford were responsible for the Northampton services. Here no. 41329 stands in a rather empty shed yard. This locomotive was fitted for push-pull working, which can be clearly seen on the front of the engine. The last of the class to be built, no. 41329 was completed at Derby in May 1952.   11.9.54

Opposite, top: Standard class 2MT no. 84020 was one of several 2–6–2Ts allocated to Llandudno shed. These engines were mostly used on local branches and station pilot work. No. 84020 was fitted for push-pull working.   16.6.63

Opposite, bottom: Two of the parallel boiler 2–6–2Ts introduced by Fowler in 1930 were to be found at Trafford Park, one of which was no. 40009. A considerable number of the 70-strong class were to be found in the London area, many of them fitted with condensing equipment for working to Moorgate.   22.9.57

In the mid-1950s Willesden was one of the largest of the London Midland Region sheds with around 143 engines, including a number of the Fowler 3MT 2–6–2Ts. No. 40019 was completed in December 1930, and is seen here fitted with equipment for motor trains.   13.11.55

The Fowler 3MT 2–6–2Ts were scattered among numerous sheds, including in the London area. This is no. 40016, a Warwick engine, photographed at Coventry.   5.2.53

Sir William Stanier introduced several locomotive designs of various wheel arrangements. In 1935 the 3MT 2–6–2Ts, a development of the earlier Fowler design, made their appearance. In all, 139 were built and distributed to depots throughout the LMS. No. 40162 is seen here (*above*) at Lower Darwen, while no. 40139 (*below*) was in good external condition at Manningham. Completed in October 1935, this engine was withdrawn in October 1959.   2.9.57/13.5.56

Bedford shed had just three 'Jinties' in its allocation during the mid-1950s. No. 47264 was one of the post-Grouping engines, a development of the Midland design with detail alterations. Completed in July 1924, it remained in service for thirty-nine years.   25.3.56

Opposite, top: Llandudno Junction was a small three-road shed. Here 'Jinty' no. 47361 stands alongside 'Royal Scot' no. 46155 *The Lancer*, with a Standard 2MT 2–6–2T in the background. By 1963, when this picture was taken, the shed had already lost a third of its allocation.   9.6.63

Opposite, bottom: Throughout the London Midland Region the ubiquitous 3F 0–6–0Ts were used as the standard LMS shunting engine. Most depots had at least one example in their allocation. No. 47361, seen here at Llandudno shed, was built in July 1926 and completed almost forty years' service. In the early 1950s just one 'Jinty' was allocated to the depot; this figure increased to three in the mid-1950s and remained so for a number of years.   16.6.63

'Jinty' no. 47373 was one of four allocated to Workington in the mid-1950s.

9.63

The 3F 0–6–0T introduced in 1924 was a post-Grouping development of the earlier Midland design. A total of 417 were built and they were distributed over a wide area. No. 47635, seen here at Normanton, was completed in December 1928 and remained in service for thirty-two years.

13.5.56

A batch of 4MT 2–6–4Ts built at Derby in 1933 were similar to the 1927 design but fitted with side-window cabs and doors. This is no. 42405 at Mirfield depot. Note the water crane with gas light above on the far side of the engine. 13.5.56

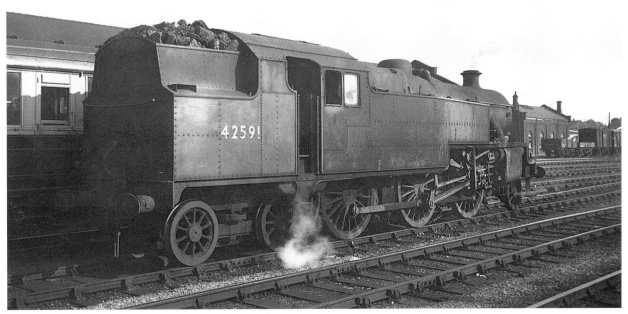

In the early 1950s motive power for the Bletchley–Cambridge services was provided by Stanier 2-cylinder 2–6–4Ts, such as no. 42591 seen here at Cambridge. These services were later handed over to Standard 2–6–4Ts. 21.7.51

In 1945 Charles Fairburn introduced a development of the well-known Stanier 2–6–4T design. One of the differences was a shorter wheelbase. No. 42699 was the last of a batch of twenty-seven engines built at Derby. Later that same year H.G. Ivatt became Chief Mechanical Engineer of the LMS. 20.3.66

Fairburn 2–6–4T no. 42064,
seen here at Trafford Park,
was completed at Derby
works in December 1950.
A considerable number of
the class were built at
Brighton.   22.9.57

Ten locomotives were allocated to Tebay shed and were mostly used for banking on Shap. Fairburn 2–6–4T no. 42110 was one of these, seen here assisting 8F no. 48136. When the summit was reached the banker would drop back, cross over and return light engine to Tebay.   9.63

Opposite, top: Tebay shed with two of the 2–6–4T bankers, a Fowler and Fairburn no. 42110. On particularly heavy trains two bankers could be required. During the 1950s and 1960s the depot had six 2–6–4Ts for this work, mostly Fairburns.   9.63

Opposite, bottom: Standard 4MT no. 80084 awaits departure time at Bletchley with a Cambridge train. These engines worked this service for several years in company with Standard 4MTs of the 75xxx series.   15.7.54

London Midland Region's Sandy station has long since gone, but it was linked to the Eastern Region main line buildings by the footbridge in the background. Standard 4MT no. 80083 is on its way to Cambridge. Note the horsebox next to the locomotive.

31.7.54

5. The Final Years

From the early 1960s it was rapidly becoming apparent that the end of steam power was in sight. Diesels were available in increasing numbers although some of the designs were to prove short-lived. There was a headlong rush to change over to diesel power, with their more comfortable and cleaner conditions also no doubt influencing this decision.

As a result most of the steam engines still in service were grubby, so much so that in some cases you could hardly read the cabside number. Maintenance suffered, despite the fact that steam was often called upon to help ailing diesels. Large areas gradually lost their steam allocation, and the northern parts of the London Midland Region were to see the final steam workings. Anyone who can remember these sad times will no doubt have happy memories of the enthusiasts' specials. The choice of motive power by this time was very limited, and one engine that was very much in demand was the newly overhauled Britannia class no. 70013 *Oliver Cromwell*. Class 5s also provided some splendid runs, and one that will long remain in my memory was no. 45407.

Anyone visiting a locomotive depot at this time would invariably find a number of withdrawn engines awaiting their final journey to a private scrapyard. These were often moved at night and their journeys were not without problems, as engines that had stood out of use for some time frequently ran hot. It was to take months before the backlog was cleared, despite the numerous private scrapyards that had sprung up in many parts of the country by this time to cut up withdrawn locomotives.

The Standard class 2MT 2–6–0s were a development of the well-proven Ivatt lightweight 1946 design. Very few changes were made other than the incorporation of BR standard fittings. The last member of the class, no. 78064, was built at Darlington and completed in 1956. The engine seen here at Crewe South under a liberal coating of soot and grime is no. 78031.   12.2.67

Two withdrawn Standard class 2MT 2–6–0s await their fate at Crewe South shed. Several condemned engines, including no. 78059 seen here, were present at this time.   12.6.67

The Ivatt 4MT 2–6–0 design first appeared in 1947 and soon proved to be a success. In due course it was used as a basis for a series of Standard 4MT 2–6–0s. No. 43024, seen here at Crewe, was completed in January 1949 and remained in service until May 1967.   12.2.67

Withdrawn engines were commonplace at many depots in 1968. Standard class 4MT no. 75034, seen here at Carnforth, had suffered considerable damage to its cylinder, while the valve gear had already been dismantled ready for the engine to make its final journey.   17.3.68

Despite its reasonable external condition, no. 44800 had been withdrawn from service and was in a siding at Lostock Hall shed. This engine was built at Derby and entered service in May 1944; it was withdrawn in March 1968, five months before the end of steam.   17.3.68

Weak winter sunshine picks out the cylinder valve gear and motion on class 5 no. 44761 at Crewe. Built at the famous locomotive works there, it entered service in October 1947 and worked until the final year of steam, being withdrawn in April 1968.   12.2.67

In the final months of steam Railway Specials were a familiar sight in the north. Here 8F no. 48476 and Standard class 5 no. 73069 run round at Hellifield, their every movement recorded by numerous cameras. 4.8.68

Opposite, top: In March 1968 Bolton shed was a shadow of its former self. Standard class 5 no. 73040 stands ready for duty. It has no shedplate but 'Bolton' has been stencilled on the buffer beam. The Lancashire & Yorkshire Railway Company originally owned this depot. 17.3.68

Opposite, bottom: The high footplate of the Standard class 5s can be clearly seen in this picture of no. 73040 at Bolton. The engine was in good external condition and no doubt would have worked enthusiasts' specials during its final months in service. 17.3.68

This picture was taken at Crewe South just nine months before the end of steam on British Railways. No. 48315 was built at Crewe in 1943. In the last years of steam many locomotives, especially goods engines, were never cleaned and most, like this one, were in a deplorable state, with grime and oil the order of the day.   12.2.67

Heaton Mersey shed was originally a Cheshire Lines depot. It had a long association with the Stanier 8F 2–8–0s, and here a work-stained no. 48267 is seen in the shed yard just a few months before steam finished on British Railways.   17.3.68

Three 8Fs, nos 48167, 48340 and 48323, stand at Rose Grove shed ready for their next duty. Time was running out as in just five months steam would be finished. 17.3.68

Manchester Victoria station was crowded with enthusiasts and onlookers when 8F no. 48476 and Standard class 5 no. 73069 worked in with an RCTS special. The last days of steam were to see many such specials, and wherever they went huge numbers of enthusiasts and members of the general public turned out to see them. 4.8.68

Many of the Standard class 9F 2–10–0s had a short working life. No. 92223, seen here at Carnforth, was among them. Had the change-over to diesel power not taken place they could have given many more years' service.   17.3.68

Many London Midland Region engines met their end in privately owned scrapyards. Class 5 no. 45302 had been towed to Cohens of Kettering, a scrapyard situated on the old Cransley branch. When engines had to be towed for some distance it was usual to dismantle the valve gear and tie the coupling rods on to the footplate. No. 45302 had been a Stoke engine.   17.3.68